Beverley Sutherland Smith

MUFFINS, CAKES
& Slices

The Five Mile Press

Metric/Imperial Measurements

In this book, quantities are expressed in metric
measures, with imperial equivalents in brackets.
These conversions are approximate only.
The difference between exact and approximate
conversions amounts to only a teaspoon
or two, and will not affect cooking results.

The Five Mile Press Pty Ltd
22 Summit Road
Noble Park Victoria 3174
Australia

First published 1998

Text copyright Beverley Sutherland Smith
Designer: Jo Waite Design
Cover design: Emma Borghesi
Editor: Maggie Pinkney
Photographer: Neil Lorimer
Production: Emma Short

Printed in Hong Kong

National Library of Australia Cataloguing-in-Publication data

Sutherland Smith, Beverley.
Muffins, easy cakes and slices
Includes index
ISBN 1 86463 051 5.
1. Baking 1. Title.
641.815

Contents

Muffins

Muffin-making is fun. You can combine all kinds of different flavours to make a wide range of muffins. They can be dense or light and airy, sweet, or savoury. Each type has its own special appeal.

Muffins are easy to make, and can be eaten hot from the oven or left to cool. They have the added advantage of reheating well. You simply wrap them in foil and place them in a preheated oven or put them on a plate in a microwave. They also freeze well.

For successful muffins, there are a few important points to remember:

- Use a non-stick baking pan. These are inexpensive and easy to clean. Butter them first, so the muffins are golden underneath.

- Always preheat the oven to moderately hot (190°C or 375°F), so the muffins will rise.

- Be sure to measure accurately. Most measurements are given in cups. A cup of flour is 155 g (5 oz).

- Sift in the dry ingredients and, when mixing through, stir or fold with a spatula. It's important to realise that muffin batter, unlike cake batter, is lumpy. It's meant to be this way. The more you mix, the greater the likelihood that the muffins will be tough and rubbery rather than smooth and soft.

- Always put the same amount of batter in each muffin-container. This way the muffins will be uniform in size and will bake at the same rate. (The following recipes make a dozen muffins, unless stated otherwise; a few make only nine.)

- To test if muffins are cooked, insert a fine skewer into the centre of one of them. If the skewer comes out clean, they are done.

If you remember these simple points you will make superb muffins.

Corn and Bacon Muffins

The natural sweetness of corn and the smoky, salty flavour of bacon make for a marvellous combination in a muffin. Makes 12 muffins.

. . . .

3 long rashers bacon, finely chopped
2 tablespoons spring onion, finely chopped
½ cup corn, scraped from a fresh cob
1 cup milk
45 g (1½ oz) butter

1 egg
2 cups plain flour
2 teaspoons baking powder
½ teaspoon bicarbonate soda
pinch cayenne pepper and salt

Method

Butter the sides and base of the muffin tins. Preheat the oven to moderately hot (190°C or 375°F). Cook the bacon in a saucepan until it is slightly crisp. Add the spring onion and corn, cover with the milk, and leave to cook over a low heat for about 10 minutes to soften the corn.
Remove from the heat. Add the butter, and leave to melt. You should have 1¾ cups of mixture. If you don't, add a little more milk. Cool. Mix with the egg.

Sift the dry ingredients into a mixing bowl. Add the corn mixture and stir until just combined. (The mixture will be lumpy, corn aside.) Spoon into the muffin tins and bake in the oven for 20–25 minutes, or until golden-brown and firm to the touch on top. Turn out onto a wire cake rack.

A quick variation

A quicker, easier version can be made using canned corn. Cook the bacon and spring onion, then add the butter to the warm pan and, finally, one cup of canned creamed corn. Add milk to make the mixture up to 1¾ cups. Cool. Then mix in the egg and continue as above.

Scraping corn from the cob, being careful not to cut in too close. This way you avoid the tough part of the corn.

Sifting the flour, salt and cayenne pepper into a mixing bowl.

The corn pieces aside, the muffin mixture has a very lumpy appearance.

Coriander and Chilli Muffins

Modern Asian flavourings are surprisingly good in savoury muffins. These could be made in miniature and served as cocktail fare. Large ones, on the other hand, are delicious with soups, stir-fries and salads, or simply as snacks. You can make these as spicy or as mild as you wish. Makes 9 large muffins, or 12 smaller ones.

. . . .

1 tablespoon olive oil
2 cloves garlic, finely chopped
1 tablespoon fresh ginger, grated
1 tablespoon sweet Thai chilli sauce
3 tablespoons coriander, choppped
1 teaspoon brown sugar

2 cups self-raising flour
1/2 teaspoon salt
60 g (2 oz) butter, chopped in small pieces
1 egg
1 cup milk

Method

Butter the sides and base of the muffin tins. Preheat the oven to moderately hot (190°C or 375°F). Heat the oil and fry the garlic and ginger for 30 seconds or until aromatic. Remove to a bowl and add the sweet Thai chilli sauce, coriander and sugar. Sift the flour and salt over the top and add the butter. Mix with your fingers until crumbly. Add the egg and milk and mix until just combined. (The mixture will look lumpy.)

Spoon into prepared tins and bake in the oven for about 20 minutes, or until well-risen and golden-brown on top. Turn out onto a wire rack.

Curried Onion Muffins with Cheese Topping

Good with almost any savoury food, or on their own, the curry mixed into the onion adds a slightly spicy flavour and the cheese gives an interesting golden coating. This makes 12 muffins.

. . . .

45 g (1½ oz) butter
2 onions, finely chopped
1 teaspoon curry powder
2 tablespoons parsley, finely chopped
1 teaspoon salt
1/2 teaspoon pepper

1 cup milk
2 eggs
additional 30 g (1 oz) butter, melted
2 cups self-raising flour
1/2 cup grated tasty cheese
1/4 cup grated Parmesan cheese

Method

Grease the base and sides of the muffin tins. Preheat the oven to moderately hot (190°C or 375°F). Melt the butter and cook the onion until soft and golden in colour. Add the curry and fry for about a minute or until aromatic. Remove and add the parsley. Season. Leave to cool.

Put into a large bowl. Add the milk, eggs and additional butter and mix. Sift the flour over the top and stir but don't over-mix. (The mixture will look a little lumpy.)

Spoon into the muffin tins. Mix both kinds of cheese together. Scatter on top of the muffins and bake in the oven for 25 minutes, or until they test cooked. Let rest for 5 minutes before removing from the tins and cooling on a wire rack.

Mushroom and Pine Nut Muffins

With the added flavours of onion and garlic, mushrooms taste very good in these savoury muffins. Darker mushrooms have more flavour than the button variety. Makes 12 muffins.

. . . .

30 g (1 oz) butter
1 tablespoon onion, finely chopped
185 g (6 oz) mushrooms, finely chopped
1 clove garlic, finely chopped
salt and pepper
⅓ cup sour cream
2 eggs

30 g (1 oz) melted butter
½ cup milk
2 tablespoons oil
⅓ cup pine nuts
2 cups self-raising flour
1 teaspoon salt
pinch cayenne pepper

Method

Grease the base and sides of the muffin tins. Preheat the oven to moderately hot (190°C or 375°F). Melt the butter in a frying pan and cook the onion for about 5 minutes or until softened. Add the mushrooms and garlic and fry until they are well cooked. Season with salt and pepper. Cook away any liquid around the mushrooms. Add the sour cream and remove to a bowl. Leave to cool and mix in the milk, eggs and melted butter. Heat the oil and cook the pine nuts until they are a pale golden colour. Drain on kitchen paper. Sift the flour over the top of the mushroom mixture, and season with salt and cayenne pepper. Stir, but don't over-mix. (The batter will look lumpy.)

Spoon into the muffin tins. Press the pine nuts on top; they will not stick if simply scattered on. Bake in the oven for 25 minutes, or until the muffins test cooked. Remove and leave for 5 minutes before cooling on a wire rack.

Blueberry, Cinnamon and Nut Muffins

Perennial American favourites, these muffins reheat very well. The blueberries provide intensely purple pockets of juicy flavour. If using frozen blueberries, allow them to defrost first and discard any liquid. Makes 12 muffins.

. . . .

2 cups self-raising flour
1 teaspoon cinnamon
1 cup castor sugar
60 g (2 oz) unsalted butter, melted

1 egg
1¼ cups buttermilk
⅓ cup pecan nuts, roughly chopped
100 g (3½ oz) fresh or frozen blueberries

Method

Grease the base and sides of the muffin tins. Preheat the oven to moderately hot (190°C or 375°F). Sift the flour and cinnamon into a mixing bowl and add the sugar. Mix the butter with the egg and buttermilk and add, along with the nuts and blueberries. Don't over-mix. Spoon the mixture into the prepared pans and bake for 25 minutes or until cooked when tested. Stand for 5 minutes before cooling on a wire rack.

Fresh Fruit Muffins

Although these muffins can be made only when fresh stoned fruit is in season, they are so exceptionally good that I have included them. Fresh apricots, plums or peaches can be used. You need to have about one cup of fresh, chopped fruit altogether to give a moist, fruity texture throughout. The sugar topping could be added to any sweet muffin. Makes 12-14 muffins.

. . . .

Muffins
125 g (4 oz) butter, cut into small pieces
½ cup thick yoghurt
1 teaspoon vanilla essence
1 cup castor sugar
2 eggs
2 cups self-raising flour
8 apricots or plums, or 4 peaches (depending on size)

Sugar topping
45 g (1½ oz) butter
2 tablespoons castor sugar
½ teaspoon ground cinnamon

Method

Grease the muffin tins. Preheat the oven to moderate (180°C or 350°F). Soften the butter with a mixer, or by hand, and add the yoghurt, vanilla and sugar. Mix well until creamy. Beat the eggs and add, a little at a time. Sift the flour over the top. Chop the fruit into pieces of about 1.25 cm (½ in) and then mix through the batter. Don't over-mix. (The mixture will be lumpy.) Spoon into the muffin tins. Bake in the oven for about 35 minutes, or until puffed on top and firm to the touch.

Remove the muffins from the containers. While they are still hot, melt the butter. Brush the top of each muffin with the butter. Sift the sugar and cinnamon over the melted butter.

Carrot and Golden Syrup Muffins

Carrot lends a moist texture to muffins, just as it does to cakes. The golden syrup adds a caramel flavour and gives a crisp crust to these excellent sweet muffins. Makes 9 large muffins, or 12 smaller ones.

. . . .

1 cup milk
2 tablespoons golden syrup
1 egg
60 g (2 oz) butter, melted
⅓ cup sugar

1 cup grated carrot
1 teaspoon grated orange rind
2 cups self-raising flour
¼ cup currants
slivered almonds (optional)

Method

Grease the base and sides of the muffin tins. Preheat the oven to moderately hot (190°C or 375°F). Mix the milk with the golden syrup, egg, butter and sugar, and stir. Put the carrot and orange rind into another mixing bowl and sift the flour over the top. Stir in the milk mixture, along with the currants, but don't over-mix. (The mixture will look lumpy.) Spoon into the muffins tins and sprinkle with slivered almonds if desired. Bake in the oven for 20–25 minutes, or until cooked when tested. These muffins become quite brown on top. Stand for 5 minutes before removing from the tins and cooling on a wire rack.

Banana Muffins

These popular muffins are especially moist and flavoursome, and keep well. Makes 9 muffins.

. . . .

2 cups self-raising flour
pinch bicarbonate soda
pinch salt
¾ cup sugar
2 large ripe bananas

45 g (1½ oz) butter, melted
1 egg
¼ cup milk
⅓ cup walnuts or pecan nuts, roughly chopped

Method

Butter the sides and base of the muffin tins. Preheat the oven to moderately hot (190°C or 375°F). Sift the flour, bicarbonate and salt into a mixing bowl. Mash the bananas and sugar together on a plate — this way the muffins will have an interesting texture. Add to the dry ingredients, along with the butter, egg, milk and nuts. Stir lightly to combine. (The mixture will be lumpy.)

Spoon into the muffin tins and bake for 20 minutes, or until golden on top and firm to the touch. Turn out onto a wire cake rack.

Low-fat Banana Muffins

Despite the fact that there is no butter or egg yolk in these muffins they are light and scrumptious, with a moist texture and good banana flavour. Makes 12 muffins.

. . . .

1½ cups plain flour
1 cup castor sugar
pinch salt
½ teaspoon baking powder
½ teaspoon bicarbonate soda
1 teaspoon cinnamon

4 egg whites
2 large ripe bananas, mashed
½ cup extra light olive oil
¼ cup low-fat yoghurt
¼ cup pecan nuts, roughly chopped

Method

Butter the sides and base of the muffin tins. Preheat the oven to moderately hot (190°C or 375°F). Sift the dry ingredients into a mixing bowl. Whisk the egg whites with a fork until broken and slightly frothy and add. Stir in the bananas, oil, yoghurt and nuts and mix lightly until just combined.

Spoon into the tins and bake for about 20 minutes or until golden and firm to the touch on top. Transfer to a wire cake rack.

Date and Lemon Muffins

The outside of this muffin is a little more crusty than usual. Inside, it is moist with dates and fresh with chopped lemon slices. It keeps particularly well. Makes 9 large muffins, or 12 smaller ones.

. . . .

3 thin slices lemon, including peel
3 tablespoons lemon juice
1/2 cup dates, chopped
1 egg
60 g (2 oz) butter, melted

3/4 cup castor sugar
1/2 cup milk
2 cups self-raising flour
1/4 teaspoon bicarbonate soda
1/2 cup pecan nuts, chopped

Method

Grease the base and sides of the muffin tins. Preheat the oven to moderately hot (190°C or 375°F). Put the lemon peel with lemon juice into a food-processor and blend until roughly chopped. Add the dates and chop, then add the egg and butter, and process until a rough paste.

Remove to a bowl and add the sugar and milk. Sift the flour and bicarbonate soda over the top and mix the batter, but don't over-mix.

Spoon into the muffin tins. Scatter the top with pecan nuts and bake in the oven for 25 minutes or until cooked. Leave to rest for 5 minutes before cooling on a wire rack.

Dried Apricot and Orange Muffins

Not too sweet, owing to the tart flavour of the apricots, this muffin could be made with prunes instead, for a breakfast treat. Makes 9 large muffins, or 12 smaller ones

. . . .

1 cup milk
2 teaspoons lemon juice
3/4 cup dried apricots, cut into small pieces
1/4 cup orange juice
3/4 cup sugar

2 cups self-raising flour
1 egg
60 g (2 oz) butter, melted
1/4 cup slivered almonds, browned first in oven
apricot jam (optional)

Method

Grease the base and sides of the muffin tins. Preheat the oven to moderately hot (190°C or 375°F). Mix the milk with the lemon juice and stand for 5 minutes. Put the apricots into a large bowl. Heat the orange juice until boiling and pour over the apricots. Add the sugar. Sift the flour over the top and add the egg, butter, milk and almonds. Mix, but not too much. (It doesn't matter if the mixture looks lumpy.)

Spoon into the prepared tins and bake for 25 minutes, or until cooked when tested. Stand for 5 minutes before cooling on a wire rack. Glaze the muffins with hot apricot jam if desired.

Grilled Capsicum and Cheese Cornmeal Muffins

Good with soup, barbecued food or a salad, these muffins have an interesting speckled appearance and cook to a good golden crust due to the combination of yellow cornmeal and tasty cheese. Makes 9 large muffins or 12 smaller ones.

. . . .

1 red capsicum
1 clove garlic, roughly chopped
¼ teaspoon cayenne pepper
6 spring onions, finely chopped
2 teaspoons brown sugar
2 cups self-raising flour

¼ cup cornmeal
½ teaspoon salt
60 g (2 oz) butter, cut into tiny pieces
½ cup grated tasty or cheddar cheese
1 egg
1⅓ cups buttermilk or milk mixed with 2
  teaspoons lemon juice

Method

Butter the sides and base of the muffin tins. Preheat the oven to moderately hot (190°C or 375°F). Cut the capsicum into halves, and remove the seeds. Place with the skin upright under a preheated griller and cook until the skin has blackened and blistered. Remove to a paper or plastic bag and allow to cool before peeling away the skin. Dice the capsicum. Mix with the garlic, cayenne pepper, spring onions and sugar.

Put the flour, cornmeal and salt into a mixing bowl. Add the butter and mix until crumbly. Now add the cheese, the capsicum mixture, the egg and milk and stir until just combined. (It will look lumpy.)

Spoon into the prepared tins and bake in the oven for about 20 minutes or until golden-brown and firm to the touch on top. Turn onto a wire rack.

Dark and White Chocolate Muffins

Chocolate muffins are among the most popular of all. They are ideal for morning or afternoon tea or as a feature of a weekend brunch. These muffins not only have chocolate inside, but also have little bits of melted chocolate on top. Makes 12 muffins.

. . . .

1¾ cups self-raising flour
2 tablespoons cocoa
½ cup sugar
60 g (2 oz) butter, melted
¾ cup milk

⅓ cup sour cream
2 eggs
60 g (2 oz) white chocolate, cut into small pieces
about 36 Choc Bits or pieces of chopped dark
  chocolate

Method

Grease the base and sides of the muffin tins. Preheat the oven to moderately hot (190°C or 375°F). Sift the flour and cocoa into a bowl. Add the sugar. Beat the butter with the milk, sour cream and eggs, and stir into the dry ingredients, along with the white chocolate. Stir, but be careful not to over-mix — it should be lumpy. Spoon the mixture into the prepared pans and bake for 25 minutes or until cooked when tested. Carefully remove from the pans to a wire rack and put three pieces of chocolate on top of each muffin. The chocolate will melt with the warmth of the freshly-cooked muffins.

Easy Cakes

There's no need to go through the messy, time-consuming process of creaming the butter for these quick and easy cakes. They are made either with melted butter or by blending ingredients for a short time in a food-processor until the colour of the batter changes slightly, becoming pale. The marvellous Light and Luscious Carrot and Nut Cake is made with extra light olive oil instead of butter.

There's a wide range of cakes, from plain buttery ones to those using more exotic ingredients such as blueberries, but all have a good light texture despite the ease of making them.

These cakes are good enough to eat as they are, with perhaps just a dusting of icing sugar over the top. However, you can ice them if you want to. Most recipes include optional icings and glazes which can be added for special occasions.

If you're unsure if a cake is cooked through you can test it by inserting a fine skewer into the centre. If the skewer comes out clean the cake is ready.

Light Chocolate Cake

With a fine sponge texture and light chocolate flavour, this cake can be creamed and served either as a dessert cake or for special occasions.

. . . .

Cake
3 eggs
⅔ cup sugar
¼ cup cocoa
½ cup self-raising flour
2 tablespoons cornflour
1 teaspoon vanilla
1 tablespoon boiling water

Filling
¾ cup cream

Topping
45 g (1½ oz) unsalted butter
2 tablespoons cocoa, sifted
2 tablespoons brown sugar
¼ cup cream
¾ cup icing sugar

To make the cake
Preheat the oven to moderate (180°C or 350°F). Butter the base and sides of a 20-cm (8-in) cake tin. Line the base with non-stick baking paper. Beat the eggs until fluffy. Gradually add the sugar and beat until thick. Sift in the cocoa, flour and cornflour and fold through. Finally, add the vanilla and boiling water, and fold again until there are no specks of flour. Spoon into the prepared tin and shake gently to level the top. Bake for about 25–30 minutes, or until firm to the touch on top. Loosen from the edges and turn out immediately onto a cake rack to cool. When cold, fill and ice.

Adding the filling
Whip the cream until stiff. Cut the cake into halves and spread the cream onto the lower half. Top with the second portion of cake.

To make the topping
Put the butter, cocoa, brown sugar and cream into a saucepan and bring to the boil. Remove from the heat. Add the icing sugar and mix well. If too firm, add a couple of tablespoons of water. Spread on some of the icing to cover the cake. Then spread on the remaining icing and smooth to the edges, so that some drizzles down the sides. You can serve the cake as it is, or decorate it with nuts, chopped peel, chocolate flakes or desiccated coconut.

Beating the eggs until really thick.

Adding the cream around the edge before smoothing over the centre, so it shows when the top half of the cake is added.

Gently pushing the icing over the edge so it drizzles down the sides.

Jamaican Fruit Cake

Any glacé fruit can be used in this American-style cake; the longer the fruit is left to marinate the better.

. . . .

1 cup sultanas

1/2 cup currants

185 g (6 oz) glacé pineapple, cut into small strips

2 tablespoons rum

3 eggs

1/2 cup brown sugar

185 g (6 oz) butter, melted and cooled

1/3 cup milk

grated rind of 1 orange

1 cup plain flour

1 cup self-raising flour

1 teaspoon mixed spice

additional rum

additional glacé pineapple pieces (optional)

Method

Butter the sides and base of a 22-cm (8½-in) cake tin. Line the base with non-stick baking paper. Preheat the oven to moderate (180°C or 350°F). Put the fruit into a basin, add the rum and stir. Leave to stand for 30 minutes. Beat the eggs with the sugar, butter, milk and orange rind. Sift both kinds of flour and the mixed spice into a basin. Make a well in the centre and add the egg mixture. Beat with a wooden spoon for 2 minutes. Add the fruit and beat again for a minute. Spoon into the prepared tin and place into the preheated oven. Bake for an hour or until the cake tests cooked. Leave to cool for an hour in the tin and then turn out, brush with rum and wrap for 24 hours before cutting. Decorate with glacé pineapple pieces if desired.

Almond Orange Cake

Ground almonds give this cake a fine texture, while the orange rind adds a moist, fresh flavour.

. . . .

Cake

185 g (6 oz) butter, cut into small pieces

grated rind of 1 orange

1 cup castor sugar

3 eggs

3 tablespoons ground almonds

1¾ cups self-raising flour

¼ cup milk

¼ cup blanched almonds, roughly chopped

Orange syrup

½ cup orange juice

¼ cup sugar

glacé oranges, cut into segments (optional)

Method

Preheat the oven to moderate (180°C or 350°F). Grease the base and sides of a 23-cm (9-in) cake tin, and line the base with a piece of non-stick baking paper. Put a third of the butter into a small saucepan and melt. Transfer to a mixing bowl and add the remaining chopped butter, the orange rind, sugar and eggs. Beat for a minute. Add the ground almonds, flour and milk and beat again for about 3 minutes. Spread into the prepared cake tin. Scatter the top with almonds. Bake in the oven for about 50 minutes to an hour, or until firm to the touch on top. Leave for 5 minutes in the cake tin before turning out onto a cake rack, almond side up. Boil the orange juice and sugar

Blueberry Cake

With a sugar-frosted top, this moist cake is studded with soft blueberries. You can use either fresh or frozen berries. If using frozen blueberries, defrost them first and discard any liquid. Frozen berries may sink to the bottom of the cake. This doesn't matter — you can simply invert the cake so they show.

Be sure the cake is cooked through before removing from the oven, as it may be brown on top but still a little undercooked in the centre. It is ready if a fine skewer inserted into the middle comes out clean. The sugar topping is optional.

. . . .

Cake
1½ cups self-raising flour
½ cup plain flour
½ teaspoon baking powder
1¼ cups castor sugar
185 g (6 oz) butter, cut into small pieces
2 eggs
½ cup buttermilk
1 teaspoon vanilla essence
250 g (8 oz) fresh or frozen blueberries

Sugar topping
30 g (1 oz) unsalted butter
2 tablespoons castor sugar
½ teaspoon cinnamon

To make the cake
Butter the sides and base of a 22-cm (8½-in) cake tin. Line the base with non-stick baking paper.

Preheat the oven to moderate (180°C or 350°F). Sift both kinds of flour into a bowl with the baking powder. Add the castor sugar. Using your fingertips, mix the pieces of butter through until crumbly.

Beat the eggs with the buttermilk and vanilla. Add this to the dry ingredients. This mixture will be stiff. Beat for a minute, and then stir the blueberries through.

Spoon into the tin and bake for about 55 minutes to an hour, or until firm to the touch on top and the cake tests cooked. Remove and leave to rest for a minute before inverting onto a wire cake rack.

To make the sugar topping
Melt the butter. Brush the top of the cake with the butter. Mix the sugar and cinnamon and scatter on top while the cake is still hot.

Leave to cool.

Light and Luscious Carrot and Nut Cake

Carrot cakes are often heavy, almost stodgy, but this one is the opposite. Light and beautifully textured, the carrot keeps this cake moist for about five days, and the combination of nuts gives an interesting texture.

You may wish to add lemon icing, but it is just as good left plain.

. . . .

Cake
⅔ cup extra light olive oil
2 eggs
1 cup firmly-packed brown sugar
1 cup self-raising flour
1 teaspoon bicarbonate soda
1 teaspoon grated lemon rind
1 tablespoon lemon juice
1½ cups grated carrot
¼ cup walnuts, roughly chopped
¼ cup pecan nuts, roughly chopped
¼ cup almonds, roughly flaked

Lemon icing
45 g (1½ oz) butter
1 tablespoon lemon juice
1 cup icing sugar

sliced almonds (optional)

To make the cake
Preheat the oven to moderate (180°C or 350°F). Butter the sides and base of a 20-cm (8-in) cake tin. Line the base with non-stick baking paper.

Put the oil, eggs and sugar into a bowl and mix. Add all the remaining ingredients except for the carrot and nuts. Beat with an electric mixer on low speed until combined and then beat on medium until the mixture has become pale in colour. Stir in the carrot and nuts.

Pour into the prepared pan. Level the top. Bake in the oven for about 45–50 minutes.

Leave to stand for 5 minutes before inverting onto a cake rack.

To make the lemon icing
Melt the butter with the lemon juice. Tip into a mixing bowl. Sift the icing sugar over the butter, and stir well. If the mixture is too runny, add a little more icing sugar, but be aware that it will firm as it cools. Pour over the cake so it drips down the sides a little.

Decorate with sliced almonds if desired.

Cherry and Chocolate Chip Cake

You will find that this cake develops a golden crust. The cherries add bright colour throughout the cake and, together with the chocolate, add enough sweetness to serve it plain.

. . . .

185 g (6 oz) butter, cut into small pieces
³/₄ cup castor sugar
¹/₃ cup milk
3 eggs
1¹/₂ cups self-raising flour

¹/₄ cup ground almonds
125 g (4 oz) glacé cherries, cut into halves
90 g (3 oz) dark chocolate, roughly chopped
icing sugar (optional)
additional glacé cherries (optional)

Method

Preheat the oven to moderate (180°C or 350°F). Butter the sides and base of a 22-cm (8¹/₂-in) cake tin. Line the base with non-stick baking paper. Put a third of the butter into a saucepan and melt. Tip into a mixing bowl and add the remaining butter. Stir until it has softened. Add the sugar, milk and eggs and beat for a minute with an electric mixer. Add the flour and ground almonds and beat on low speed for a minute, or until the ingredients are combined. Now beat on medium speed until the mixture has changed colour and is smooth. It takes about 3 minutes. Add the cherries and chocolate. Spread into the tin and bake in the oven for about 50 minutes to an hour, or until firm to the touch on top. Leave to stand for 5 minutes before inverting onto a cake rack to cool. Decorate with sifted icing sugar and glacé cherries if desired.

Orange Marmalade Cake

The marmalade adds a rich tartness to this cake. Orange, cumquat or mixed citrus can be used.

. . . .

Cake
¹/₃ cup marmalade
grated rind of 1 orange
125 g (4 oz) butter, cut into small pieces
1 cup self-raising flour
¹/₂ cup sugar
2 eggs
¹/₂ cup pecan nuts, roughly chopped

Marmalade icing
¹/₃ cup orange marmalade
30 g (1 oz) unsalted butter
1 cup icing sugar

Method

Butter the sides and base of a 20-cm (8-in) cake tin. Line the base with non-stick baking paper. Preheat the oven to moderate (180°C or 350°F).

Warm the marmalade with the orange rind. Remove from the heat and add the butter. When melted, stir well and put into a mixing bowl. Leave to cool for a minute. Sift the flour over the top and add the sugar, then beat in the eggs and nuts. Stir well with a wooden spoon for a minute or until very well blended. It will be a stiff mixture. Spoon into the prepared tin and smooth the top. Bake in the oven for 35 minutes or until it tests cooked. Leave to cool in the tin for 5 minutes, then invert onto a wire rack. Warm the marmalade until bubbling on the edges, remove and add the butter and stir well. Transfer to a mixing bowl. Sift the icing sugar over the top and leave for a minute until it firms slightly, then spread over the top of the cake.

Old-fashioned Chocolate Cake

A big cake suitable for family gatherings, it keeps well for days. Nice plain, but even better iced.

. . . .

Cake
2 cups self-raising flour
2 cups sugar
5 eggs
³⁄₄ cup milk
125 g (4 oz) butter, melted
¹⁄₃ cup cocoa

Chocolate icing
45 g (1¹⁄₂ oz) butter
2 tablespoons cocoa
2 tablespoons milk
2 cups icing sugar
desiccated coconut

Method

Butter the sides and base of a 25-cm (10-in) cake tin. Preheat the oven to moderate (180°C or 350°F). Put all the cake ingredients into a mixing bowl and beat with an electric beater for a minute on low, or until the ingredients are blended. Then beat on medium speed for 3 minutes. The mixture should become lighter in colour as it is mixed. Spoon into the prepared tin and bake in the oven for 45 minutes, or until firm to the touch on top and a fine skewer inserted into the centre comes out clean. Leave to cool for 5 minutes in the tin before inverting onto a cake rack. Melt the butter. Sift the cocoa into the butter and add the milk. Bring to the boil. Mix in the icing sugar until you have a smooth mixture, adding more milk as necessary. Spread over the cake, leaving little peaks, and scatter with coconut.

Apricot Boiled Fruit Cake

Canned fruit adds flavour and keeps this boiled fruit cake moist for about ten days.

. . . .

425 g (about 1 lb) canned apricot halves
1 cup sultanas
¹⁄₂ cup currants
¹⁄₂ cup mixed peel
¹⁄₂ cup glacé cherries
³⁄₄ cup brown sugar
1 teaspoon bicarbonate soda
2 eggs
1 teaspoon vanilla

1 cup plain flour
1 cup wholemeal self-raising flour
¹⁄₂ teaspoon mixed spice
¹⁄₂ teaspoon nutmeg
1 teaspoon cinnamon

¹⁄₂ cup apricot jam (optional)
dried apricots (optional)

Method

Butter the sides and base of a 22-cm (8¹⁄₂-in) cake tin. Line the base with non-stick baking paper. Preheat the oven to moderately slow (160°C or 325°F). Chop up the apricots into pieces. Put the apricots and their juice into a saucepan with the mixed fruits and sugar. Bring very slowly to the boil and leave to simmer for 5 minutes. Remove from the heat, add the bicarbonate soda and stir. Let cool. Beat the eggs and mix through with the vanilla. Put into a bowl. Sift both kinds of flour with the spices over the top and mix with a wooden spoon. Put into the cake tin and bake for about 1¹⁄₄ hours or until the cake tests cooked. Brush the top of the cake with hot apricot jam, and decorate with dried apricots. These can also be glazed with apricot jam.

Slices

Slices can be exotic or quite simple and homely in style but, whichever kind you make, a slice is one of the most useful of sweet delights to keep in the house. You can cut them into big pieces for hungry teenagers or into small wedges, diamonds, squares or strips according to your fancy. Sliced into tiny pieces they can be served as *petits fours*, to go with after-dinner coffee.

Don't worry if you don't have a tin of the exact size mentioned in a particular recipe — just use one of a similar size, if you have it. If you only have a large shallow baking pan you can pack one end with crumpled tinfoil, and then place a straight edge of foil along the side to reduce the area used. This trick works really well, and means you only need to have one or two tins to make slices.

Most slices keep well in an airtight container, and are ideal for packing into school lunches or for taking on picnics and family outings.

Lemon Coconut Slice

The buttery base is topped by a lemon sour cream custard. Although it may appear very soft on top, even after baking, the topping will firm more as it cools and has a wonderful creamy, lemon flavour.

. . . .

Base
1½ cups self-raising flour
¾ cup sugar
grated rind of 1 lemon
⅓ cup desiccated coconut
125 g (4 oz) butter, cut into small pieces
1 egg
1 tablespoon milk
1 tablespoon lemon juice

Topping
½ cup apricot jam
1½ cups sour cream
2 eggs
3 tablespoons lemon juice
¾ cup castor sugar

To make the base

Butter the sides and base of a shallow tin, 30 x 20 cm (12 x 8 in). Preheat the oven to moderate (180°C or 350°F).

Sift the flour into a bowl and add the sugar, lemon rind and coconut. Add the butter and work through the mixture with your fingers until it is crumbly.

Beat the egg, milk and lemon juice, and add to the mixture. Knead.

Alternatively, you could make the base in a food-processor. First, put the flour, sugar, lemon rind, coconut and butter in the bowl and blend until crumbly. Then add the egg, milk and lemon juice, and process until the mixture forms a ball.

Either roll out between waxed paper and place in the tin, pressing the mixture up the sides, or simply press into the tin in pieces, again making sure it goes right up the sides.
Bake in the oven for 30 minutes, or until firm and a light golden colour.

To make the topping

Warm the apricot jam and pour over the top of the crust. Spread out gently. Mix all the remaining ingredients into a bowl, stirring well. It will look very liquid. Pour over the base and return to the oven. Cook for about 15 minutes or until set on top.

When cool, cut into strips or squares.

Pressing the mixture onto the base and up the sides of the tin.

Gently spreading the warm apricot jam.

Pouring the remaining ingredients over the jam.

36

Nut and Sultana Slice

Crisp and buttery, this slice needs no topping. But be sure to pack it well down into the tin when you bake the mixture, so it will not be too crumbly.

. . . .

185 g (6 oz) butter
³/₄ cup firmly-packed brown sugar
¹/₂ cup pecan nuts, roughly chopped
¹/₂ cup hazelnuts or almonds, roughly chopped

1 cup sultanas
¹/₂ cup desiccated coconut
1 egg
1 cup plain flour

Method

Butter the sides and base of a shallow 22-cm (8¹/₂-in) cake tin. Preheat the oven to moderate (180°C or 350°F). Slowly melt the butter and when bubbling on the edges remove and mix in the brown sugar. Tip into a mixing bowl. Add the nuts, sultanas, coconut and egg. Stir well. Sift the plain flour over the top and mix. Put into the tin and press down firmly and evenly, using a damp wooden spoon or moistened hands. Bake for 25 minutes, or until firm to the touch and a pale golden-brown. Leave to cool in the pan. Keep for 12 hours before cutting into strips or squares when cold.

Golden Brownie Slice

If you like the flavour of caramel and chocolate you will love this brownie, which is rather like fudge in the centre.

. . . .

Base
1¹/₃ cups brown sugar
100 g (3¹/₂ oz) unsalted butter, cut into pieces
2 eggs
1 cup plain flour
1 teaspoon baking powder
pinch salt
185 g (6 oz) chocolate, cut into small pieces
¹/₂ cup walnuts or pecan nuts, roughly chopped

Chocolate truffle icing
¹/₄ cup cream
30 g (1 oz) unsalted butter
100 g (3¹/₂ oz) milk chocolate, cut into small pieces
¹/₄ cup walnuts or pecan nuts, finely chopped

Method

Preheat the oven to moderate (180°C or 350°F). Butter the side and base of a shallow cake tin, 28 x 18 cm (11 x 7 in), and line the base with non-stick baking paper. Put the sugar and butter into a saucepan and melt over a low heat. When the edges of the mixture are boiling remove and let cool for 10 minutes. Beat the eggs until frothy, add the butter and sugar, and mix well. Sift the flour with the baking powder and salt over the top and stir. Mix in the pieces of milk chocolate and walnuts and spoon into the prepared pan. Bake for 20 minutes, or until it is risen on the edges and firm to the touch in the centre. It will firm more as it cools. Leave to cool in the tin.

Heat the cream with the butter until it is boiling. Remove from the heat and add the chocolate. Stir slowly until melted. Pour onto the top of the brownie slice and spread to the edges. Scatter with the nuts. Leave to cool completely before cutting into strips or squares.

Coconut Apricot Slice

In this variation on an old-fashioned favourite, the buttery brown sugar base is topped by jam and a coconut crust, with almonds for additional texture. Easy to make, it keeps very well.

. . . .

Base
1 cup plain flour
¹/₃ cup brown sugar
100 g (3¹/₂ oz) butter

Topping
³/₄ cup apricot or raspberry jam
2 egg whites
¹/₃ cup castor sugar
1 cup desiccated coconut
¹/₃ cup almonds, chopped

Method

Butter a shallow 22-cm (8¹/₂-in) square pan. Preheat the oven to moderate (180°C or 350°F). Sift the flour into a bowl and add the sugar. Cut the butter into small pieces. Process all the ingredients in an electric blender. Press firmly into the pan. The mixture will be a little crumbly.

Warm the jam. Spread over the top of the base. Beat the egg whites in a bowl until they form stiff peaks. Gradually add the sugar and beat for a minute. Mix in the coconut and nuts and spread over the apricot jam. Bake for about 25–30 minutes, or until the top is golden and the base is firm. Cool in the pan and cut into strips or squares.

Chinese Chew Slice

There appears to be no rhyme or reason for the unusual name given to this slice. Made from an old and not-so-well-known English recipe, it has a sticky, slightly chewy centre and a firm, cracked, crusty top, giving a marvellous contrast of textures. It keeps well for at least a week.

. . . .

2 eggs
1 cup sugar
1 cup dates, finely chopped
1 cup walnuts, roughly chopped
³/₄ cup plain flour

¹/₂ teaspoon baking powder
pinch salt
1 teaspoon vanilla
30 g (1 oz) melted butter

Method

Butter the sides and base of a shallow tin, 28 x 18 cm (11 x 7 in). Line the base with non-stick baking paper. Preheat the oven to moderate (180°C or 350°F). Beat the eggs until fluffy, add the sugar, and beat again for a minute. Mix in the dates and walnuts. Sift the flour, baking powder and salt over the top and mix through with the vanilla and, lastly, the melted butter.

Put into the tin and bake for 25–30 minutes, or until golden-brown on top and firm to the touch. The top will form little cracks, rather like a meringue when it is cut.

Dried Apricot and Chocolate Chip Slice

This delicious slice keeps well for a week, is simple to mix and is very popular.

. . . .

Base
200 g (7 oz) dried apricots, cut into quarters
¾ cup brown sugar
½ cup water
125 g (4 oz) butter, cut into small pieces
½ teaspoon bicarbonate soda
2 eggs
1 cup plain flour
pinch salt
½ cup buttermilk or milk with 2 teaspoons lemon juice added

185 g (6 oz) milk chocolate, finely chopped
¼ cup walnuts, chopped
Icing
60 g (2 oz) unsalted butter
2 tablespoons lemon juice
2 cups icing sugar
2 tablespoons grated dark chocolate

Method
Butter the sides and base of a shallow tin, 30 cm x 20 cm (12 x 8 in). Preheat the oven to moderate (180°C or 350°F). Heat the apricots with the brown sugar, water and butter until the butter is melted and the mixture is bubbling at the edges. Remove to a large basin and add the bicarbonate soda. Let cool for 3 minutes. Beat the eggs. Add to the mixture. Sift the flour and salt over the top and add the buttermilk, chocolate and nuts. Mix well with a wooden spoon for a minute. Spoon into the prepared tin and smooth the top. Bake in the oven for 25–30 minutes, or until firm to the touch. Leave to cool. Mash the butter until soft. Add the lemon juice and then the icing sugar. Mix well. Spread over the apricot base. Scatter with the grated chocolate. Cut into strips or squares.

Marshmallow Slice

The base of this slice has a buttery, chocolate flavour, offset by a marshmallow topping.

. . . .

Base
1 cup self-raising flour
1 tablespoon cocoa
⅓ cup castor sugar
¼ cup coconut
155 g (5 oz) butter, melted

Marshmallow topping
½ cup desiccated coconut
1 x 500 g (1 lb) packet pink or white marshmallows
½ cup milk
additional desiccated coconut

Method
Butter the base of a shallow pan, 30 x 25 cm (12 x 10 in). Preheat the oven to moderate (180°C or 350°F). Mix the flour, cocoa, sugar, coconut and melted butter and press over the base of the buttered pan. Bake in the oven for 20 minutes, or until firm to the touch. Remove and cool before spreading with the marshmallow topping. Put the coconut into a dry frying pan, and stir until a pale golden colour. Remove and cool. Put the marshmallows into a saucepan with the milk. Cook over a low heat, stirring constantly until the marshmallows have melted. Cool slightly and pour onto the base. Top with coconut and leave to set. Cut into squares.

Chocolate Walnut Brownies

Rich, sticky in the centre and with a light crust on top, this dark chocolate brownie slice is very easy to make. It is ideal cut into tiny pieces as *petits fours*, or to accompany tea or coffee at any time of day. The chocolate frosting is optional.

. . . .

Base
185 g (6 oz) dark chocolate, roughly chopped
125 g (4 oz) butter, cut into small pieces
$\frac{1}{2}$ cup brown sugar
$\frac{1}{2}$ cup castor sugar
1 teaspoon vanilla essence
2 eggs
1 cup plain flour
$\frac{1}{2}$ cup walnuts, roughly chopped

Fudge frosting
60 g (2 oz) unsalted butter
$\frac{1}{4}$ cup cream
100 g (3$\frac{1}{2}$ oz) dark chocolate, cut into small pieces
1 teaspoon vanilla essence

To make the base
Butter the sides and base of a shallow 20-cm (8-in) square cake tin. Line the base with non-stick baking paper.

Preheat the oven to moderate (180°C or 350°F).

Put the chocolate and butter into a bowl over a saucepan of simmering water and leave until melted. Transfer to a large bowl.

Add both kinds of sugar, the vanilla and the eggs and beat until blended. Sift the flour over the top and stir through with the walnuts.

Spoon into the prepared tin and smooth the top. Bake for about 25–30 minutes, or until firm to the touch on the edges and just barely set in the centre.

Cool in the pan and carefully invert onto a board. Ice if you wish, and cut into squares or slices.

To make the fudge frosting
Warm the butter and cream until bubbling. Remove from heat. Add the chocolate and stir until smooth. Add the vanilla.

Pour over the slice and smooth the top. Leave to set.

Orange Oat Slice

Chock-a-block with oats and sweetened with golden syrup, this wholesome slice has a chewy texture, rather like a muesli bar. It keeps particularly well.

. . . .

1 cup rolled oats
²/₃ cup plain flour
¹/₃ cup self-raising flour
1 cup castor sugar
³/₄ cup desiccated coconut

¹/₃ cup mixed peel, chopped
125 g (4 oz) butter, chopped into small pieces
1 tablespoon golden syrup
1 teaspoon grated orange rind
2 tablespoons water

Method

Grease a shallow 28- x 18-cm (11- x 7-in) pan and line the base with non-stick baking paper, extending it over the rim. Mix the oats, flour, sugar, coconut and mixed peel in a bowl. Put the butter into a small saucepan, and melt. Then add the golden syrup, orange rind and water. Stir, then tip into the oat mixture and continue stirring thoroughly until blended. Press into the lined pan, using the heel of your hand. The firmer you press, compacting the mixture, the better the texture will be.

Bake in a moderate oven (180°C or 350°F) for about 25–30 minutes, or until golden on top and firm to the touch. It will harden more as it cools. Leave to cool in the pan and then remove by lifting on the paper. Cut into squares for storing, using a sharp knife to give straight edges.

The Mars Bar Slice

This ever-popular slice keeps best refrigerated, so it remains crisp. A mix of caramel and chocolate, with the crunch of Rice Bubbles, it is ideal for parties.

. . . .

Base
3 x 65 g (2 oz) Mars Bar, roughly chopped
90 g (3 oz) unsalted butter
3 cups Kellog's Rice Bubbles

Topping
185 g (6 oz) white chocolate, roughly chopped
30 g (1¹/₂ oz) unsalted butter
3 tablespoons cream
¹/₂ cup desiccated coconut or nuts, finely chopped

Method

Butter the base and sides of a shallow tin, 25 x 20 cm (10 x 8 in). Put the Mars Bars with the butter in a large saucepan. Cook over a low heat, stirring constantly until the mixture has melted and is smooth. Use a whisk to mix; it is difficult to get smooth otherwise. Remove from the heat and mix in the Rice Bubbles. Spoon into the tin and spread out evenly, using the back of a dessertspoon which has been quickly dipped into water. Press down slightly and leave to cool and set.

Put the white chocolate, butter and cream into a bowl and leave to melt over a saucepan of simmering water. Spread over the Mars Bar slice and scatter with coconut or nuts. Let cool. Store this refrigerated. Cut into squares or strips.

Acknowledgements

The author and publishers are grateful to David Jones, Bourke Street, Melbourne, for the loan of china, glassware and table linen.
The author also wishes to thank Gwenda Bailey and Pat McDonald for their help in preparing the test recipes, and Diane McCormick for keying the manuscript.

Index